Tanri

Financial and Accounting Audit

Abdelmounim Bouziane
Wadi Tahri

Financial and Accounting Audit

Development of a monitoring dashboard for the
implementation of audit recommendations

LAP LAMBERT Academic Publishing

Imprint

Any brand names and product names mentioned in this book are subject to trademark, brand or patent protection and are trademarks or registered trademarks of their respective holders. The use of brand names, product names, common names, trade names, product descriptions etc. even without a particular marking in this work is in no way to be construed to mean that such names may be regarded as unrestricted in respect of trademark and brand protection legislation and could thus be used by anyone.

Cover image: www.ingimage.com

Publisher:
LAP LAMBERT Academic Publishing
is a trademark of
Dodo Books Indian Ocean Ltd. and OmniScriptum S.R.L publishing group

120 High Road, East Finchley, London, N2 9ED, United Kingdom
Str. Armeneasca 28/1, office 1, Chisinau MD-2012, Republic of Moldova, Europe

ISBN: 978-620-7-46019-9

Copyright © Abdelmounim Bouziane, Wadi Tahri
Copyright © 2024 Dodo Books Indian Ocean Ltd. and OmniScriptum S.R.L publishing group

Financial and Accounting Audit

Development of a monitoring dashboard for the implementation of audit recommendations

Foreword

We are delighted to present this collaborative work, "Financial and Accounting Audit: Development of a monitoring dashboard for the implementation of audit recommendations." As authors, our backgrounds complement each other, with one specializing in the intricate field of audit and the other in management and quality.

The dynamic landscape of financial auditing necessitates constant adaptation to emerging challenges. In this book, we delve into the critical intersection of financial audit practices and the development of a cutting-edge monitoring dashboard. Our goal is to provide valuable insights and methodologies that bridge the gap between audit recommendations and their effective implementation.

As practitioners and researchers in our respective fields, we recognize the importance of integrating the latest advancements in both audit methodologies and management practices. Through our collaboration, we aim to offer a comprehensive guide that not only addresses the complexities of financial auditing but also provides a tangible solution – the monitoring dashboard.

This book is the result of meticulous research, practical experience, and a shared commitment to advancing the realms of audit and management. We extend our gratitude to those who have contributed to our journey, and we hope that this work serves as a valuable resource for professionals, academics, and students alike.

Thank you for joining us on this exploration of the evolving landscape of financial and accounting audit.

Abdelmounim Bouziane
Wadi Tahri

Table of Contents :

- General Introduction 5
- PART I: FINANCIAL AND ACCOUNTING AUDIT 7
  - Chapter I: Introduction to Financial and Accounting Audit 8
  - Historical overview of the evolution of audit: 9
  - Logic and typology of financial and accounting audit: 11
  - Chapter II: Challenges of Financial and Accounting Audit Missions 21
  - 1-Steps for conducting financial and accounting audit work 22
- PART II: FOLLOW-UP OF RECOMMENDATIONS FROM FINANCIAL AND ACCOUNTING AUDIT MISSIONS. 26
  - Chapter I: The progress of the audit mission 27
  - 1-the presentation phase 29
  - Implementation phase: 35
  - 3-The Conclusion Phase: 40
  - Chapter III: Development of a dashboard for monitoring recommendations .. 42
  - Work context: 43
  - 2-Presentation of the dashboard for monitoring recommendations 45
- General Conclusion: 53
- Appendix 55
  - Appendix 1: (Opinion Report) 56
- Bibliography: 61

"Excellence is not an act, it is a habit."
- Aristotle

General Introduction

Business leaders and organizations today recognize the crucial importance of understanding their environment in order to anticipate future developments and make informed decisions. The ability to correctly interpret the reality that surrounds them guides the direction of their choices, whether that reality concerns the environment, markets, products, or financial resources. This in-depth understanding is imperative for making wise decisions.

The relevant analysis of this reality, whether it is the global environment, dynamic markets, innovative products, or crucial financial resources, becomes a priority for companies seeking to excel. Although financial and accounting instrumentation plays an essential role in facilitating the analysis of the multiple data that flow into the company's environment, it is essential to emphasize that this analysis may sometimes not accurately reflect the desired reality.

In the absence of rigorous external control, anomalies and errors can creep into financial statements, compromising their fidelity. It is in this context that financial and accounting audit emerges as an effective solution to remedy this situation. It involves a thorough examination of the evidential matter justifying the data contained in the accounts, evaluating the accounting principles applied and the significant estimates used, while examining the overall presentation of the accounts.

In Morocco, the use of audit has become widespread, leading to the creation of numerous specialized firms in recent decades. These firms carry out financial audit missions for companies, issuing opinions on the regularity, sincerity, and fidelity of the accounts. This trend reflects an increasing importance placed on transparency and trust in the Moroccan economic context.

Audit firms undertake missions to detect anomalies and risks that could compromise the continuity and sustainability of the audited structures. The conclusions of these missions are the subject of an audit report that holds the auditors responsible. In order to optimize the efficiency of the firm, it is crucial to establish a rigorous follow-up of the implementation of the recommendations formulated in the audit report. It is with this objective in mind that this book details the necessary steps to monitor the implementation of the remarks made during a legal audit mission.

The first and second chapters will cover generalities about the field of accounting and financial auditing, including the definition, stages, objectives, participants, etc. The second part will be devoted to presenting the progress of an audit mission, followed by the exposition of the techniques to be put in place to ensure the monitoring and evaluation of the implementation of the auditor's recommendations.

PART I : ACCOUNTING AND FINANCIAL AUDIT

Chapter I :
Introduction to Accounting and Financial Audit

1- Historical overview of the evolution of auditing :

Although the term may seem recent, the concept of auditing is actually very ancient. The initial form of auditing is manifested through accounting and financial auditing, also known as statutory auditing (Gaddour, 2016).

Indeed, the evolution of economic structures and large administrative and commercial organizations has been accompanied by the development of accounting control practices (Pierre Loyer, 2006). It is from the 19th century that these practices have experienced systematic development, in parallel with the emergence of the modern enterprise. It is during this time that auditing gradually took on the form it currently has.

Furthermore, accounting and financial auditing has undergone methodological evolution. At its beginnings, the auditor carried out a comprehensive check of all entries recorded in the journal (Reference). However, this approach posed problems of exhaustiveness, which led to the adoption of a systems-oriented approach. This approach consisted of evaluating internal control systems on the assumption that any malfunction at this level would have an impact on the quality of the accounting records and, consequently, on the overall quality of the accounts.

In order to control the costs of audit missions, auditors sought an approach that reconciles the maximization of assurance and reliable results with reduced costs. This dual challenge was achieved with the risk-based approach, which breaks down the accounting and financial audit mission into 3 main phases:

❖ Knowledge acquisition phase: which allows the auditor to seek elements of understanding to identify risk areas and frame his work for the next phases;

❖ Internal control evaluation phase: based on the risk areas defined in the knowledge acquisition phase, the auditor seeks presumptive elements. This phase allows the auditor to determine the extent of his investigations at the third phase level.

❖ Examination of accounts phase: which allows the auditor to gather sufficient evidence to judge the quality of the accounts.

Also, in order to minimize costs, companies have considered training salaried accountants so that they can assume a large part of the tasks traditionally carried out by statutory auditors. Consequently, statutory auditors spend less time on auditing, resulting in a decrease in billed fees.

The role played by the salaried accountant or internal auditor within the accounting and financial function has been widely recognized, which has prompted companies to seek their services for other functions. This has led to the emergence of internal auditing in the true sense of the term, covering all of the company's activities.

It should be noted that the difference between external accounting and financial auditing and internal auditing is manifested in the fact that for the former, the evaluation of internal control is a means to frame the extent of its investigations, while for the latter, it is an end in itself.

From a historical point of view, the emergence of internal auditing finds its justification in the desire to reduce the costs associated with statutory auditing missions, especially in large companies.

In Morocco as well, accounting and financial auditing as currently organized and practiced is part of the same global dynamic. It meets the need to ensure the accuracy of the accounts, to cope with the increase in the volume of information, and to face environmental pressure marked by increasingly intense competition.

Indeed, for a successful Moroccan business takeover, it is necessary to carry out various audits that will allow for a fair evaluation and, above all, to minimize the risks inherent to the target company. Consequently, several efforts by the Moroccan government, jointly initiated by the World Bank and the International Monetary Fund (IMF), have been deployed to focus on the strengths and weaknesses of the accounting and auditing environment that influence the quality of published financial information (Hazami-Ammar, 2018). The measures adopted in this framework involve reviewing legal obligations and practices, and consider international financial reporting standards (IFRS), international standards on auditing (ISA), as well as internationally accepted practices in the field of accounting regulation and auditing, including the main provisions of European law (the acquis communautaire).

2- Logic and typology of accounting and financial auditing :

Like any type of audit, accounting and financial auditing is the starting point of a process that allows the auditor to establish a diagnosis. This diagnosis then serves as a basis for identifying improvements and formulating recommendations that will be implemented. Thus, accounting and financial auditing plays an essential role in identifying improvement opportunities and optimizing the accounting and financial practices of the company. In particular, accounting and financial auditing is an examination of the company's financial statements, aiming to verify their accuracy, regularity, compliance, and ability to reflect a true and fair view of the company (Portal, 2011):

-Accuracy: it results from the correct evaluation of accounting values, as well as a reasonable application of risks and impairments by the management; loyalty and good faith in the preparation of the accounts.

-Compliance: with legislation and international standards in force.

-Regularity: accounts in compliance with internal regulations.

-True and fair view: reflects the concept of "true and fair view". The notion of a true and fair view is linked to the obligations of regularity and accuracy, as well as the application of the principle of prudence.

2-1- General logic of accounting and financial auditing:

Audit is defined as "the professional examination of information in order to express a responsible and independent opinion on this information with reference to a quality criterion, this opinion must enhance the usefulness of the information".[1]

From this definition, we can identify the pillars of any audit mission: professional examination, independence, reference, and usefulness of the information.

---

[1] Bernard Germond, financial audit, 1996.

The professional examination concerns the methodology followed when examining a company's accounts, as every auditor uses methods and techniques while respecting the professional requirements of the profession.

Similarly, among the conditions for the success of an audit mission, there is the independence and neutrality of the audit in relation to the audited entity. No link should exist between the representatives of the examined company and the persons in charge of the mission, hence ensuring the reliability and sincerity of the information and conclusions made by the audit team. And the responsible opinion entails civil and criminal liability for the auditor.

The basis of an audit or review is the reference for the mission, i.e., the standards against which the auditor will certify or not certify a company's accounts.[2]

At the end of the audit mission, and in the case of certifying the accounts (with or without reservation), the information included in the financial statements and management reports of the company will have credibility and will be accepted and shared by partners and third parties, thus increasing their usefulness.

The audit focuses on analyzing the internal control practices implemented by the company, as well as analyzing the main transactions and operations in relation to a framework in order to reveal existing discrepancies, seek explanations, their causes and consequences on the reliability of financial information, and propose actions to correct them.[3][4]

Financial auditing is carried out in relation to internal or external frameworks, and therefore it can be characterized as a compliance audit.

Compliance audit is "the professional examination of information in order to express a responsible and independent opinion on this information with reference to a quality criterion; this opinion must enhance the usefulness of the information".[5]

---

[2] For a mission of accounting and financial audit, the standards primarily consist of accounting standards and standards related to the profession.
[3] All the security measures and frameworks implemented by the company under its responsibility.
[4] The threshold (in amount or percentage) beyond which any deviation is likely to impact the company's accounts.
[5] Financial Audit and Compliance Audit Manual, European Court of Auditors, 2012.

Similarly, the statutory audit is different from the contractual audit, as it is a mission that certain companies must carry out by force of law.[6]

In the context of a statutory audit, the statutory auditor must ensure to shareholders, partners, and the State that the accounts prepared and presented by the management give a true and fair view of the financial position of the audited entity.

The mission is called statutory because it is legally mandatory for companies that meet certain conditions, especially in terms of legal form (SA, certain SAS and SARL, and even associations) and according to the level of turnover achieved in the past financial year. The statutory auditor is appointed by the AGM for a period of 6 financial years. In certain cases, companies are required to appoint both an auditor and a co-auditor. Another clarification to make is that statutory audit is an external audit, or in other words, a third-party audit. The distinctive feature of an external audit is essentially based on the independence of the body responsible for the audit mission from the audited entity, hence the credibility and reliability of the conclusions.

Three main concepts form the basis of financial accounting audit:

- Financial information: refers to the financial data and reports analyzed to assess the reliability, compliance, and relevance of a company's financial statements. These financial statements are the result of recordings and entries in appropriate accounts, following a given presentation and displaying balances as of the closing date (interim or final). The aim here is to highlight the fundamental relationship between financial information (the subject of financial audit) and the production apparatus of financial information, in other words, the administrative and accounting organization of the company.
- Financial information aiding investors in making investment decisions: The financial accounting audit intervenes at this level to compare the reality of the company and the communicated financial information (the notion of true and fair view).

---

[6] L'audit contractuel désigne les missions qu'un CAC ou expert-comptable peut mener pour une entreprise afin de répondre à un besoin bien déterminé.

- The life of the company (its activity, structure, general policy, the culture of its managers, its development prospects, and its administrative and accounting organization) is constantly exposed to a series of risks (commercial failure in a market or product, strategic failure in political choices, organizational failure in structures, administrative and accounting failure in management systems...) that can lead to the ultimate risk of business cessation. Here, we highlight the danger that a company may face if it does not undergo a permanent evaluation of the quality of the financial information it believes it controls.

From another perspective, audit, depending on its nature, is an approach to risks that leads to an evaluation of the probability of failure of an organization or its functioning. Therefore, audit work must necessarily focus on the most critical aspects of the company, also known as the company's risk areas; they fall into three categories:

- Company risks: associated with the economic and financial situation of the company, they may include elements such as the economic situation of the sector in which it operates, the nature of the products or services sold, and changes in physical infrastructures.
- Management risks: stemming from the overall organization of the company, they include elements such as the absence of regularly updated procedures and function definitions, the absence of an internal audit function, and deficiencies in human resources management.
- Accounting risks: related to accounting organization and management; Risk elements in this context may include the failure of the accounting control system, whether in its design or operation, as well as the complexity of accounting transaction processing and valuation issues. Therefore, during an audit of the accounts, it is at most possible to detect significant failures and ask the auditor to provide reasonable assurance that there are no major anomalies. It can be deduced that any audit act inherently carries a level of risk of error (which the auditor acknowledges and the auditee accepts).

On the other hand, determining a materiality threshold is essential for the financial auditor to focus on the most important aspects in their work and to assess whether the errors and failures detected are likely to call into question the certification and whether it is appropriate to request the company to correct its financial statements.[7]

The significance threshold in auditing represents a fundamental element that guides auditors in their evaluation of an entity's financial statements. This threshold is defined as the level beyond which errors, omissions, or distortions in the financial statements could have a significant impact on users' decision-making. It is crucial in the planning and conduct of audit work as it allows auditors to determine the extent of procedures to be implemented to obtain reasonable assurance about the reliability of financial information. Setting the significance threshold involves careful analysis of the risks inherent in the entity's activities, industry characteristics, and specific regulatory environment. A well-defined significance threshold provides auditors with a solid basis for identifying areas of significant risk, selecting audit samples, and formulating informed opinions on the reliability of financial statements. In summary, the significance threshold is an essential parameter that guides the rigor and relevance of audit procedures, thereby contributing to the integrity and credibility of the financial audit process.

In the end, the financial auditor is subject to an obligation of means and not results. (Lherm, 2013) They are not required to have absolute certainty about the accounts, but rather to provide reasonable assurance regarding the absence of significant errors in the financial statements.

2-2- Typology of accounting and financial auditing :

Accounting and financial auditing, as an essential discipline for ensuring transparency and reliability of financial information, takes on different forms and typologies depending on its objectives, organizational context, and specific needs of stakeholders.

---

[7] "Materiality threshold: a measure taken by the financial auditor of the amount beyond which one or more errors or inaccuracies, when cumulated, impact the financial statements in such a way that they are no longer fair and true or no longer provide a faithful representation of the assets or results of the operations of the entity in question." - Financial and Operational Audit, ALIRAQUI.

These different categories of auditing offer a diversity of methodological approaches and focuses to address the multiple dimensions of risk management and financial compliance.

External auditing stands out as one of the most well-known and widely practiced typologies. Carried out by independent experts, external auditing aims to certify the truthfulness and compliance of an entity's financial statements. This form of auditing serves to enhance the confidence of external stakeholders, such as investors, creditors, and regulators, by ensuring that an entity presents a true picture of its financial position. External auditors examine the accounts, evaluate internal controls, and form an opinion on the quality of financial information, thereby contributing to the stability of financial markets.

In contrast, internal auditing is a typology that focuses on evaluating internal processes within an organization. Conducted by professionals internal to the entity, internal auditing aims to improve operational efficiency, assess compliance with internal policies, and identify potential risks. This form of auditing acts as an internal management tool, providing recommendations to strengthen internal procedures, optimize resources, and ensure compliance with applicable regulations. Internal auditing also contributes to the promotion of a robust internal control culture within the organization.

Another significant typology of auditing is operational auditing. This type of auditing focuses on evaluating operational activities and business processes within an organization. The primary objective of operational auditing is to optimize operational efficiency, identify gaps in processes, and propose tangible improvements. This form of auditing often examines aspects such as human resource management, logistics, and information systems, thereby providing a comprehensive view of the entity's operational performance.

Compliance auditing also stands out as a specific typology, focused on verifying compliance with applicable laws and regulations. This form of auditing ensures that the entity complies with the legal obligations governing its industry. Compliance auditors evaluate documentation, procedures, and practices of the organization to ensure they are in line with current legal standards, thereby reducing legal risks and potential sanctions.

Financial auditing can also be segmented into financial performance auditing and budget management auditing. Financial performance auditing focuses on evaluating the profitability, liquidity, and solvency of an organization. Financial performance auditors examine financial statements to assess the financial health of the entity and make recommendations to improve the use of financial resources. On the other hand, budget management auditing focuses on evaluating the planning and budgetary control of the organization, contributing to ensuring effective allocation of resources and achieving financial objectives.

Finally, environmental auditing is emerging as a specialized typology, focused on evaluating the environmental impacts of an organization's activities. This type of audit examines compliance with environmental standards, assesses environmental risks, and proposes measures to minimize the entity's ecological footprint. Environmental auditing reflects the growing concern for sustainability and corporate social responsibility.

In brief, we can summarize the different typologies of financial and accounting auditing as follows:

• **Internal financial and accounting auditing:**

This is an audit performed by an employee of the company itself, with the aim of ensuring the quality of financial and accounting information. Its objective is to provide an opinion on the compliance, accuracy, and fidelity of the financial statements. The three traditional levels are distinguished:

❖ Compliance audit:

- Evaluate compliance with the standards required by the country.
- Verification of the dates of recording of accounting transactions.
- Verification of the amounts of provisions.

❖ Efficiency audit:

- Verify the efficiency and simplicity of work procedures, especially in terms of information flow.

- Evaluate the smoothness of information transmission between the accounting and finance department and the administration.

- Evaluate the competencies of the personnel in the accounting department.

❖ Management audit:

- Verify the mechanisms that allow managers to make strategic choices, control financial performance, and make necessary corrections.

• **External financial and accounting auditing:**

It is common for certain third parties or partners with links to the company to request that the accounts be examined before making important decisions. Thus, the request for an audit can be made by:

- Banks,
- Employees, through the committee or unions,
- A company wishing to merge,
- The State,
- Shareholders...

Therefore, external financial and accounting auditing has two main types:

❖ Legal or certification audit:

Legal audit is an obligation provided for by current legislation, for public establishments, joint-stock companies, limited liability companies, and joint-stock companies. Legal audit can be recurring or one-time.

Recurring legal audit is entrusted to the professional by the assembly (or equivalent body) within the framework of a renewable three-year mandate, in one of the following forms:

- Legal review of accounts, for public establishments.
- Statutory audit, for private companies or those with public participation.

One-time legal audit is entrusted to the professional by the assembly (or equivalent body) within the framework of a one-time mission according to legal requirements:

- Contribution audit, in the case of contribution in kind.
- Merger audit, in the case of company merger.
- Diagnostic audit, in the case of transformation of the company's legal form.

❖ Contractual audit:

The request for this control can be made by the company or by third parties. This control must comply with the standards of the Order of Chartered Accountants. Any financial and accounting information can have serious consequences for the company, so it is necessary for managers to ensure the accuracy of the information. The concerns of a review for managers are often:

- The need for reliable financial information before presenting it to third parties or shareholders.
- Assessing the current accounting organization to identify deficiencies and improve them.
- The need to prevent fraud and misappropriation.

Contractual audit is an "open" mission that allows the company to benefit from high-value-added services in the following areas:

- Business valuation in the context of external growth or restructuring operations (including if the target company already has an auditor).
- The analysis of the quality of the firm's information system: to secure it and improve its reliability,
- The evaluation of assets or liabilities: within the framework of targeted operations
- The evaluation of specific risks, etc..

We are therefore talking about contractual audit, insofar as this intervention takes place within a contractual framework and is freely defined between the Statutory Auditor and his client.

Although it is no longer within the scope of the statutory audit, the Statutory Auditor is required to comply with the working standards of the profession and its Code of Ethics.

Indeed, the accomplishment of his mission requires the implementation of rigorous and diligent procedures that allow for the provision of high value-added services.

The terms and scope of the contractual audit are defined by the parties (the client and the professional) within the framework of a contract negotiated on a case-by-case basis (engagement letter). It can cover the following work:

- Audit assistance: assistance to the company in preparing its financial statements
- Consolidation audit: due diligence with subsidiaries or other holdings in the case of assistance in the preparation of the consolidated financial statements (accounts) of the parent company or holding company.
- Transmission audit: due diligence with companies to be sold or acquired in the context of privatization, acquisition, sale, partial asset contributions
- Diagnostic audit: in the context of corporate restructuring
- Investigation audit (investigation)
- Procedures & systems audit

Chapter II:
Challenges of Accounting and Financial Audit Missions

1-Stages of carrying out accounting and financial audit work

Accounting and financial audit represents a crucial step in the transparent and efficient management of companies, aiming to guarantee the reliability and integrity of their financial statements. This complex process takes place in several methodical stages, each playing an essential role in verifying the accounts and detecting any anomalies. The first major step in this process is the evaluation of internal control and its techniques. This phase involves a thorough analysis of the mechanisms and devices put in place by the entity to ensure the validity and security of financial information. The techniques used at this stage make it possible to detect any weaknesses or gaps in the internal control system, thus providing a solid foundation for the rest of the audit.

Once the evaluation of internal control is completed, the second stage focuses on the control of accounts and its techniques. This phase includes a meticulous review of the company's transactions, balances, and accounting operations. The techniques used at this stage include confirmation of balances with third parties, physical inspection of assets, analysis of income statements and balance sheets, as well as comparison of financial data with industry standards and expectations. These procedures aim to identify any errors, omissions, or possible fraud, thus providing assurance as to the accuracy of the presented accounting information. The combination of these two stages constitutes a robust foundation for a comprehensive audit, offering a reliable overview of the financial health of an organization. The steps followed in the conduct of financial and accounting audit missions are as follows:

❖ **Evaluation of Internal Control:**

In-depth analysis of the mechanisms of internal control in place.

Identification of strengths and possible weaknesses.

Evaluation of the effectiveness of control policies and procedures.

Use of techniques such as workflow analysis and authorizations.

❖ **Control of Accounts and Associated Techniques:**

Confirmation of balances with third parties and business partners.

Physical inspection of tangible assets and assessment of their condition.

Detailed analysis of income statements and balance sheets.

Comparison of financial data with sectoral standards and expectations.

- ❖ **Risk Assessment:**

Identification of potential risks related to operations and financial statements.

Evaluation of the probability and impact of these risks on the reliability of the information.

Implementation of specific procedures to mitigate identified risks.

- ❖ **Substantive Tests:**

Execution of detailed tests to verify the validity of transactions and balances.

Use of techniques such as statistical sampling to ensure representative coverage.

Identification and thorough investigation of detected anomalies.

- ❖ **Communication with Management:**

Regular exchanges with management to clarify any questions.

Obtaining additional information about processes and transactions.

Feedback on preliminary findings and possibility of proactive correction.

- ❖ **Audit Report:**

Compilation of audit findings and conclusions.

Issuance of a detailed report on compliance and reliability of financial statements.

Recommendations for improving accounting practices and internal control, if applicable.

2-standards of accounting and financial audit work :

Accounting and financial audit is based on a set of standards and principles that rigorously govern the conduct of this crucial practice for transparency and reliability of financial information within organizations. These standards aim to ensure the objectivity, independence, competence, confidentiality, and integrity of auditors, while establishing clear guidelines for the conduct of audit work. One of the preeminent standards in the field of audit is the International Audit Standard (IAS), issued by the International Federation of Accountants (IFAC). These international standards establish a commonly accepted framework, ensuring a consistent and quality approach to the conduct of audit missions worldwide.

The first fundamental standard in the field of audit is that of professional integrity. Auditors must demonstrate unwavering honesty and objectivity in the performance of their duties, avoiding any potential conflicts of interest that could compromise their independence. This standard also emphasizes the importance of confidentiality, requiring auditors to preserve the confidential nature of the information obtained during their mission. This is particularly crucial for instilling stakeholders' trust in the audit process.

Another key standard concerns professional competence and professional judgment. Auditors must possess the technical skills required to successfully carry out their audit missions, which includes a thorough understanding of accounting standards, internal control principles, and audit techniques. Additionally, they must demonstrate sharp professional judgment to critically evaluate financial information, identify risks, and formulate informed conclusions.

Independence is also a cardinal principle in auditing. Auditors must be free from any external influence that could compromise their objectivity. This standard aims to ensure that auditors' opinions and conclusions are not biased by inappropriate relationships or pressures, thus ensuring that the audit report faithfully reflects the financial reality of the audited entity.

Audit standards also include specific guidelines regarding the planning and execution of audit work. Rigorous planning is essential to determine the appropriate scope of work and identify areas of significant risk. This phase involves a thorough understanding of the audited entity, its environment, its industry, as well as the definition of an appropriate audit strategy. The execution of work, on the other hand, encompasses the collection of sufficient and appropriate audit evidence to support auditors' conclusions. This step requires the implementation of various procedures, such as compliance tests, substantive tests, and the evaluation of accounting estimates.

Documentation is another fundamental standard in the field of audit. Auditors must comprehensively and accurately record all relevant information regarding the planning, execution, and conclusions of the audit. This documentation provides a clear record of the work performed, facilitating the supervision and review of audit missions, while serving as a reference for potential future revisions.

The communication of audit findings is also regulated by specific standards. Auditors must clearly and objectively present their conclusions in a formal audit report. This report, intended for internal and external stakeholders, must include an opinion on the compliance of financial statements with applicable accounting standards, as well as comments on accounting practices, internal controls, and any issues identified during the audit.

Furthermore, audit standards are constantly evolving to adapt to changes in the business world, regulatory changes, and technological advancements. Auditors are required to stay informed of recent developments and update their skills accordingly. Continuous training and professional development are therefore essential elements to ensure compliance with constantly evolving audit standards.

In conclusion, the standards of accounting and financial audit work play a central role in preserving the integrity and credibility of the audit process. These standards, whether issued at the international or national level, aim to instill stakeholder confidence by ensuring rigorous, independent, competent, and ethical audit practices. By diligently following these standards, auditors contribute to strengthening the quality of financial information, thereby supporting stability and trust in financial markets.

PART II : FOLLOW-UP OF RECOMMENDATIONS FROM FINANCIAL AND ACCOUNTING AUDIT MISSIONS.

Chapter I:
The conduct of the audit mission.

The conduct of a financial and accounting audit mission is a complex and methodical process that aims to assess the reliability and compliance of an entity's financial statements. This approach, essential for ensuring transparency and stakeholder trust, follows a set of key steps, from initial planning to communication of audit findings. One of the first steps is mission planning. Auditors must understand the entity, its environment, objectives, as well as the inherent risks in its activities. This in-depth understanding serves as a basis for determining the scope of the mission, identifying areas of significant risk, and formulating an appropriate audit strategy.

Planning also includes evaluating the entity's internal control. Auditors examine the systems, policies, and procedures of internal control in place to ensure their effectiveness in preventing and detecting potential errors or fraud. This evaluation of internal control guides the design of subsequent audit procedures and optimizes the efficiency of audit work.

Once planning is complete, auditors move on to the execution phase of the work. This step involves collecting sufficient and appropriate audit evidence to support the auditors' conclusions. Techniques used include compliance tests to assess the reliability of internal control systems, substantive tests to verify the validity of transactions and balances, as well as analytical procedures to identify trends and anomalies.

As part of the execution of the work, auditors may also choose statistical sampling to assess an entire population based on a representative sample. This technique saves time while providing reasonable assurance that the results obtained from the sample apply to the population as a whole.

Auditing accounts often involves auditing cycles, which examine essential accounting cycles such as sales, purchases, cash, fixed assets, etc. Each cycle is evaluated based on its relative importance and associated risks. This cycle approach allows auditors to focus on critical areas while ensuring comprehensive coverage of financial statements.

Ongoing communication with management is a crucial aspect during the execution of the work. Auditors exchange information with management to clarify any issues, obtain clarification on accounting practices, and share preliminary observations. This collaboration promotes mutual understanding and contributes to the quality of the audit.

Following the execution of the work, auditors move on to the synthesis and analysis phase of the results. They gather findings, assess the impact of detected anomalies, and form conclusions on the reliability of the financial statements. This phase also includes an evaluation of accounting estimates, post-closing events, and other aspects that may influence financial results.

Documentation of the entire process is an essential standard. Auditors must record in detail all stages of the mission, the procedures followed, the results obtained, as well as discussions with management. Documentation provides a clear record of the work performed, facilitating supervision, review, and future revisions.

The synthesis phase leads to the drafting of the audit report. This formal document presents the auditors' conclusions, their opinion on the compliance of the financial statements with accounting standards, as well as recommendations to improve accounting practices and internal controls if necessary. The audit report is generally addressed to internal and external stakeholders, providing assurance on the quality of the financial information presented by the audited entity.

Finally, the last step of the audit mission involves communicating the results to stakeholders. Auditors discuss their findings with management, answer any questions, and provide clarifications on points raised during the mission. This transparent communication strengthens stakeholder confidence in the audit process and provides valuable insights to management to enhance financial management of the entity.

1- Presentation phase

1-1- Mission order:

Every financial audit mission begins with an engagement letter, which formalizes the mandate given by the management to the firm.

This letter specifies the conditions for carrying out the mission, as well as the accounting framework that will serve as the basis for the verifications and possible treatments. The engagement letter is also an opportunity for the firm to request unconditional collaboration from the management and all individuals who may hold useful information for the auditors.

The letter also indicates an estimate of the firm's fees and the payment conditions for these fees.

1-2-Understanding and Familiarization with the Entity:

This step involves gaining knowledge of the regulatory, accounting, and business sector environment. It aims to better understand the characteristics of the entity, its categories of transactions, account balances, objectives, and strategies implemented to achieve them. The auditor acquires this knowledge through the study of external documentation (general and specific data and regulations : international, national, sectoral environment) and internal to the company (procedures, organizational charts, strategic plan), direct contacts (interviews with executives and various departmental managers), and site visits.

The general familiarization with the company is an opportunity to reacquaint oneself with the various actors in the entity. The auditors had the following objectives :

- To have an overall view of the entity and the internal controls implemented to manage it.
- To identify the most significant risk areas in order to not overlook fundamental aspects later on or conversely, not get lost in unnecessary details.
- To define the objectives of the mission based on the findings and risk areas in order to then be able to plan, organize, estimate the cost and time of the mission
- To present a good image of rigor and professionalism in order to create an atmosphere of trust and facilitate contact.

Indeed, the auditors first proceeded to verify the existence of the internal control system. Thus, the engagement partner scheduled a series of interviews with the personnel of the department to test whether the description of the internal control corresponds to reality.

Then, the team selected a typical transaction from the purchasing and sales procedure flowchart to follow it throughout its diagram, verifying that the described operations are in line with reality. The supports used during this step are as follows:
- Search for internal documentation: procedures manual, ...
- Interviews with key personnel and site visits
- Identification of internal IT tools
- Examination of legal documents

In parallel, to identify the areas where the most damaging risks are likely to occur, the team used a grid of combinatorial risk factors that can be of three types:
- Inherent risk: defined as the risk that an account or category of transactions contains significant isolated or cumulative anomalies with anomalies in other balances or categories of operations, regardless of existing internal controls. This may involve risks related to the business sector, regulations, or the complexity of operations.
- Control risk: defined as the risk of not detecting an anomaly in an account or category of operations despite the accounting and internal control systems implemented in the entity, therefore due to the entity's own systems.
- Detection risk: defined as the risk that the substantive procedures implemented by the auditor fail to detect errors in an account or category of operations, therefore specific to the audit approach.

Thus, the risk analysis grid is presented as follows:

Table 2: Risk Analysis Grid1

Level of diligence		Control risk		
		High	**Medium**	**Low**
Inherent risk	**High**	Maximum	High	Medium
	Medium	High	Medium	Low
	Low	Medium	Low	Minimum

In addition, the auditors also use a risk assessment questionnaire, which is quantified on each line and results in an overall assessment for the section (shaded area); the risk is considered: high (H), medium (M), or low (L).

Table 3: Risk Assessment Questionnaire2

	Risk assessment
Business-related risks	⇨
⇨ Business sector (in growth or in recession)	
⇨ technological and business development capacity	
⇨ product and market specific risks	
⇨ integrity and competence of management	
⇨ management influencing factors	
⇨ management interest in accounting and financial data	
⇨ degree of fragility of financial structure	
⇨ compared ratios of company and industry average	
⇨ compliance with laws and regulations	
⇨ degree of awareness of fraud and error risk	
⇨ existence and number of regulated agreements	

⇨ difficulties between or with partners	
⇨ assessment of business continuity	
⇨ identification of payment delays	
⇨ quality of the company's general organization	
⇨ existence of a manual of appropriate procedures and documentation	
⇨ staff skills	
⇨ place of external stakeholders	
off-balance sheet commitments ⇨ existence of significant commitments or lack of information literacy	
general audit risk	⇨

A more detailed approach in terms of audit assertions is then developed by the team after analyzing the information collected during this questionnaire, which leads to the following grid:

Table 4: Audit Grid3

Qantifications H = high M = medium L = low	Completeness	Existence	Rights and duties	Assessment	Measurement	Affiliation	Presentation	Significance
Sales/customers								
Purchasing/suppliers								
Borrowing loans								
Staff								
Intangible & tangible assets								
Treasury								
Tax aspects								
Stocks and inventory								

1-3- Mission Plan.

The management held an inaugural meeting with the auditors, during which discussions took place to clarify certain aspects related to the approach and implementation of the project.

− Not only focus on the problematic aspects, but also highlight the existing strengths.

− When conducting audits, it is essential to take into account the specificities of the public sector, both in terms of compliance with current regulations and various aspects related to internal control.

- Adopt the following cyclical approach, which allows for a coherent and logical integration of the income statement accounts:
    - Clients/billing/sales
    - Cash/banking
    - Investment and fixed assets
    - Personnel/payroll
    - Inventory and stock
    - Purchases/suppliers
    - Loans/borrowings
    - Tax aspects

Regarding the structure of the report, it was specified that the firm should present three types of reports:
- Accounts report
- Opinion report
- Internal control report

This working meeting allowed for the finalization of the contract and the operations schedule.

2- Implementation phase :

2-1- Evaluation of internal control:

The various institutional definitions given to internal control can be summarized by the following characteristics:
- Set of methods and procedures
- Aim to organize business activities
- Aim to safeguard the company's assets
- Prevent and detect irregularities and inaccuracies
- Ensure the accuracy and completeness of accounting records
- In accordance with management's instructions and in pursuit of performance improvement

At this level, the auditors have integrated internal control into their mission as follows:

- Understanding of procedures: By using an approach that combines a series of interviews with the heads of the accounting and finance department, examination of procedure manuals, system mapping (in the form of narration and/or diagrams), and procedure testing, we seek to evaluate the implementation of procedures.
- Evaluation of internal control: The objective is to identify both strengths and weaknesses regarding audit risk issues. The identified strengths are subject to permanence tests to ensure their value over time.
- Utilization of the evaluation of internal control: By establishing a connection between the evaluation of internal control and the accounts control program, which complements the risk measurement.

2-2- Audit of accounts:

The initial verifications carried out concern the opening balances, as they constitute a fundamental basis for comparison and reconciliation. To do this, the auditors have included in the mission due diligence to ensure:

- that the opening balances do not contain any anomalies that have a significant impact on the financial statements of the current period
- that they have been correctly carried forward
- that the closing and valuation methods of the accounts have been consistently applied; if not, any changes must be mentioned and quantified in the ETIC.

The auditors then proceed with accounting estimates contained in the financial statements. Accounting estimates are approximate evaluations of the amount of an item in the absence of a precise measurement method; the following are targeted:

- provisions for impairment of receivables or inventory
- prepaid income or expenses
- provisions for risks and charges
- warranty provisions
- losses on long-term contracts
- deferred taxes

These are estimates whose triggering event can be punctual or recurrent. The techniques used are as follows:
- Examination and testing of the procedure followed by management to make the estimate (and compliance with the consistency of methods for recurrent terms)

- Use of an independent method to make a comparison
- Examination of subsequent events to confront the estimate

The next step consists on the assessment of evaluations. These are the evaluations recorded or mentioned in the ETIC. The team's approach in this context includes the following steps:
- Understanding the methods adopted by the company for these evaluations and the reference values used
- Identification of the participants in the evaluation process (internal and external, human and computer)
- Assessment of the appropriateness of the choices made and their implementation (particularly in relation to the applied accounting framework)
- Possible use of an expert
- Assessment of the determined values, the calculation assumptions used, and the information provided in the financial statements regarding these
- Assessment of the validity of the methods chosen in relation to the overall situation of the entity, its strategy, and the information obtained during the engagement

The auditors then proceed to verify compliance with the principle of continuity of operations. Continuity of operations is a fundamental accounting convention; therefore, it is important for the auditor to ensure that the entity is still able to maintain this principle.

In general, accounting frameworks create an explicit obligation regarding this principle; the auditor examines this in the specific case of the controlled entity.

As far as we are concerned, this principle has been verified through the analysis of certain indicators, including:

- Level of equity and working capital
- Gross operating margin
- Operating gain or loss
- Insufficient cash to pay creditors on time
- Credit refusal by suppliers
- Shortage of essential raw materials

Thus, auditors base their controls and verifications on the assurance that the entity complies with the accounting principles that form the core of accounting.

The following table summarizes the examinations conducted by the team.

Table 5: Audit examination conducted by auditors4

Concern	Principle	Verification	Risk
recordings	completeness	Sum of actual transactions = Sum of accounting records	actual > accounting
	reality	Sum of accounting entries = Sum of actual transactions	Accounting > actual
	exercise separation	Sum of accounting entries for the fiscal year = Sum of actual transactions for the fiscal year	Actual (y) > accountign (y) Accounting (y) > actual (y).
Balance	existence	Asset and liability balances = Existing assets and liabilities	unjustified balance

	accurate assessment	balances values = fair values	overstated balance or understated balance
Financial documents	compliant presentation	presentation in compliance with the current accounting framework	Bad classification
	Information	Additional necessary information	unreported change

Note: It should be noted that, in addition to the traditional tools and techniques used in an audit engagement, such as sampling analysis, interviews, and observation, the team also used direct confirmation (or circularization). This method allows for obtaining information directly from third parties in relation to the company's transactions. The level of evidence obtained in this way can be considered reliable, as it allows for verifying the reality and completeness of the transactions.

The approach of direct confirmation :

- Circularization is generally carried out on the closing date of the company's financial statements, but it can also be done at any other time. In any case, the chosen reference period must be clearly indicated on the circularization request.
- The selection of third parties to be subject to circularization must be done in a way that ensures a sufficient number of responses to guarantee the reliability of the approach: therefore, a representative number of third parties and the values involved (in movement or balance). This should not lead to a selection based solely on significant balances, for example; thus, reversed balances or zero balances can be validly included in the sample selected.
- The auditor must present the entity with the list of information requests that he plans to send in order to obtain its agreement. In case of disagreement, the auditor will

have to implement additional means of investigation (although their evidential value may not be equivalent) and assess the potential impact on his engagement in terms of limitations.

3- Conclusion Phase:

3-1- Synthesis of audit work:

This summary focuses on the extent of the work carried out and highlights the errors and inaccuracies identified that have not yet been addressed by the company.

At this stage, the team has verified the completeness of the necessary work, meaning that they have been able to carry out all the work they deemed relevant.

Next, the identified errors and inaccuracies were summarized and their adjustments examined. The auditors then compared the total amount of adjustments to the materiality threshold defined at the beginning of the engagement.

3-2-Audit reports and the auditor's opinion:

As known, the external financial auditor is required by law to prepare a general report and issue their opinion on the financial statements.

As a reminder, it is important to note that the firm has committed to providing the management with three types of reports: the accounts report, the opinion report, and the internal control report.

The accounts report aims to present the findings and strengths identified during the audit work, thus providing a comprehensive diagnosis of the various cycles and formulating recommendations to improve the control of accounting operations. As for the internal control report, it aims to highlight the quality of the center's internal control system by conducting a detailed analysis of the accounting procedures and evaluating compliance with accounting principles, which form the basis of accounting.

The opinion report, on the other hand, has the main mission of presenting the auditor's opinion on the truthfulness and regularity of the center's financial statements, thus certifying the reliability of its accounts.

The structure of the report is as follows:

- The title (audit report)

- The recipients of the report (shareholders and the board of directors)
- The identification of the annual accounts (company name, closing date of the annual accounts, and the period they cover)
- The fact that the financial statements are prepared under the responsibility of the company's management and that the auditor's role is to express an opinion on these statements.
- Details on the extent of the audit work:
  - Reference to audit standards or accepted practices
  - Mention that the audit aims to obtain reasonable assurance
  - The opinion on the annual accounts, which must be clearly expressed and mention the reference frameworks of the accounting principles and methods used for the preparation of the financial statements
  - The auditor's signature, address, and date of the report
  - In summary, it should be noted that the audit engagement results in the preparation of a working paper file, which serves as:
  - Both a framework for conducting the engagement (audit planning and execution)
  - A tool facilitating the supervision and review of the audit work
  - And a support justifying the performed procedures and gathering the evidential matter supporting the auditor's opinion.
  - It can be materialized in paper or electronic format; it includes:
  - The tools of the approach (such as questionnaires, templates, diagrams)
  - The working notes of the audit team (engagement partner and staff)

NB: See an example of the structure of the audit file in the appendix.

Chapter III : Development of a dashboard for monitoring recommendations

1- Work context :

The idea of publishing a book on the development of a dashboard for tracking recommendations from a legal audit mission represents a relevant and crucial initiative in the field of governance and financial control. Such a book could provide a comprehensive guide, offering audit professionals and financial managers the necessary tools to establish an effective system for monitoring recommendations made following an audit mission. It would be able to explore the different stages of the process, from the formulation of recommendations to their implementation, with an emphasis on the importance of proactive management of corrective actions. This would enable organizations to improve their governance by ensuring the implementation of appropriate corrective measures and compliance with current standards and regulations. Furthermore, such a book could address best practices for designing clear, accessible, and results-oriented dashboards, thereby facilitating continuous monitoring of progress and enabling a transparent evaluation of the effectiveness of actions taken. In summary, a detailed guide on the development of a dashboard for tracking legal audit recommendations could be an invaluable resource for strengthening corporate governance and promoting a culture of accountability and continuous improvement.

1-1- Interest and general logic of the project :

In Morocco, the emergence of auditing as a distinct discipline has gradually manifested itself over the past few decades, reflecting the transformations of the global economy. The country's businesses, faced with leadership challenges, intense competition, and a complex economic situation, find themselves in increasing need of relevant tools to optimize their activities and demonstrate their performance to external stakeholders.

Auditing provides a reliable method for assessing the current situation of a company. By identifying areas of competence and areas requiring improvement, it serves as a mechanism for control and validation. This critical dimension strengthens the position of auditing as a contemporary control instrument.

If we specifically focus on external auditing, which focuses on the certification of financial statements, certain aspects may question the integrity of auditing as a process.

However, it is evident that auditors invest significant effort to ensure the success of their missions. Their approach includes a thorough familiarization with the relevant context, meticulous planning of audit activities, rigorous verification, and the formulation of relevant recommendations. Unfortunately, the majority of audit entities neglect the follow-up of issued recommendations, even though auditing, by its nature, should stimulate concrete actions.

Faced with this reality, the envisaged book aims to establish a system for monitoring audit recommendations issued following an official audit mission. The ambition is to create a dedicated dashboard that will act as an evaluation instrument for audited entities and auditors themselves. Through specific indicators, this dashboard will provide audited entities with a perspective on the impact of the audit and an assessment of the effectiveness of auditors' interventions. At the same time, it will offer auditors an opportunity to measure the effectiveness of the implementation of their recommendations.

1-2-General logic of the project :

Numerous studies have sought to understand audit quality (Chemingui and Pigé, 2004). This has been approached either through the analysis of auditor quality (following DeAngelo's work, 1981) or based on the analysis of the audit process.

Nevertheless, evaluating or measuring this quality presents difficulties. Indeed, the result of audit quality is not directly or immediately visible : the audit process is very complex and not observable by third parties, while the audit report, as the result of the audit, is often standardized in its content and formulation, offering little opportunity for distinction.

In this perspective, it is possible to consider that the evaluation of audit quality can be done by following the implementation of recommendations resulting from audits and evaluating their contribution to improving the accounting system of the audited entity. Therefore, this work consists of designing a dashboard for monitoring the implementation of audit recommendations and their effectiveness, accompanied by a tracking sheet for these recommendations, serving as a basis for information collection.

In summary, two tools are proposed :
- The dashboard : This instrument allows for the evaluation of the effectiveness of recommendations using a sample of indicators that offer the possibility to measure the relevance of recommended actions.
- The follow-up sheet for the implementation of actions resulting from audit work : This is a sheet designed to collect the necessary information for feeding the dashboard.

These tools are of significant importance for both auditors and auditees. Indeed, they will allow the auditee to ensure the proper implementation of audit recommendations and evaluate their contribution to improving work methods and the internal control system.

For the auditor, these tools will serve as after-sales service to the client by measuring customer satisfaction through the evaluation of the effectiveness of recommendations once implemented. This will enable the firm to improve its work methods and report writing in order to facilitate the understanding of recommendations. The objectives of recommendation monitoring can be summarized as follows :
- For the auditor: By monitoring recommendations, the auditor will be able to provide after-sales service to the client by assisting them in implementing the proposed actions. Furthermore, this will allow them to assess the practical effectiveness of these actions, with a view to improving future services and better meeting client expectations.
- For the auditee : To enable a better evaluation of audit results by assessing the various stages of recommendation implementation and their effectiveness.

2-Presentation of the recommendation monitoring dashboard :

Before presenting this instrument for evaluating the effectiveness of recommendations resulting from audits, it seems necessary to first define the concept of a dashboard, its usefulness, and its instruments.

2-1-Concept of the dashboard :

What is a monitoring dashboard ?

The monitoring dashboard, in its theoretical conception, brings together a set of indicators that are regularly updated and used to track the evolution of a system. These indicators act as alerts, automatically triggering to signal any anomalies or performance in the functioning of the system (Savignat, 2014).

Indeed, the dashboard is inherently designed as a control and comparison tool. However, the information system it encompasses also plays an essential role as a communication tool, promoting dialogue, and as an aid to decision-making.

Furthermore, a management dashboard consists of a selection of indicators that allow a manager to monitor the evolution of results and compare deviations from reference values such as set objectives, internal or external standards, or statistical references, as close to real-time as possible, focusing on those that are considered most significant.

NB : There is no standard model for a dashboard. It is a personal instrument, designed to measure the responsibilities and objectives of its user.

What is the purpose of a monitoring dashboard ?

Just like the dashboard of a vehicle that provides crucial information such as speed, fuel level, oil level, and the status of lights, the management dashboard serves the same function. It provides real-time indications to the user about the reliability, efficiency, and effectiveness of their entire system. Thus, as soon as an element presents a defect or deviation, the user is immediately informed.

What are the instruments of the monitoring dashboard ?

The dashboard is essentially based on a set of indicators that must have certain characteristics to better represent the information.

To understand the concept of an indicator, let's start with a definition : an indicator is an element or combination of elements that represents the state or evolution of a system. It is selected based on the actions to be taken and the decisions to be made in the future. Indicators are chosen to provide relevant information for identifying action levers and taking necessary corrective measures.

In parallel, there are other instruments often used in the dashboard, including :

- Deviations : budgetary control allows for the calculation of a number of deviations. It is then a matter of identifying the one or ones that are of interest to the recipient of the dashboard.
- Ratios : these are reports of significant magnitudes of the company's operation.
- Graphs : they allow for visualizing trends and highlighting changes in pace or direction.
- Indicators : these are threshold limits defined by the company and considered as action variables. Their exceeding obliges the responsible person to take action and implement corrective measures.

2-2-Design of the dashboard for monitoring the effectiveness of actions :

The design of the dashboard will be approached in two phases :

The first phase : objectives and indicators of the dashboard

At the beginning of this preliminary phase, we focus on defining the objectives to be achieved. Once these objectives are clearly defined, we proceed to the selection of relevant indicators that adequately reflect the effectiveness of the recommendations and contribute to the achievement of the predetermined objectives. Indeed, as the crucial objective of all companies is to produce an image capable of reflecting to the public the state of its assets and results. This image must therefore be faithful to its source and also be as close as possible to the reality of the company.

The recommendations made by auditors play a crucial role as a guide for continuous improvement of accounting practices. Regardless of the specificities and relevance of these recommendations, their ultimate goal is to meet fundamental objectives :

- Consistently apply accounting principles, namely :
    - Continuity of operations ;
    - Consistency of methods ;
    - Historical cost ;
    - Period specialization ;
    - Prudence ;
    - Clarity ;

- ▪ Materiality.
- Timely declare complete and accurate financial statements indicating the true situation of assets and liabilities and a clear view of profits and losses for the period
- Respect deadlines for declaring value-added tax to the tax authorities in order to minimize losses incurred from late filing penalties.
- Respect the completeness and chronological order of accounting records.
- Formalize all procedures related to the accounting and financial system.

The indicators of the efficiency dashboard :

The choice of indicators will be oriented towards achieving the above-mentioned objectives and will be selected based on the criterion of relevance.

Here is an example of indicators that can be selected :

•Average time for declaring financial statements

•Reliability rate of financial statements (in terms of substance and form)

•Completeness rate of records (calculated as follows) :

$$\frac{\text{Balance of actual records - sum of accounting records}}{\text{Sum of the records for the fiscal year}}$$

•Degree of formalism of accounting procedures

The above indicators are just a reference example. The choice of indicators remains relative to the set objectives and the expectations of the audited company. In any case, an indicator must be :

√Easy to understand, measure, and represent ;

√Limited in number, otherwise they cannot be used as decision-making tools ;

√Measured at a frequency linked to improvement possibilities ;

√Implemented and generalized quickly.

The second phase : presentation and use of the dashboard :

- Presentation of the efficiency dashboard of recommendations ;
- Use of the efficiency dashboard of recommendations ;
- The designed dashboard will allow its user to have a clear view of the level of effectiveness of the recommendations proposed by auditors through three basic tables ;
- Indeed, as shown in the image above, the first table is used to measure the degree of effectiveness of the recommendations while ensuring the monitoring of their implementation. Therefore, the first column will include the proposed actions, the second will be reserved for measuring their implementation by indicating the percentage of their application during the planned period, while the third column will be dedicated to measuring the effectiveness of these actions. Thus, the recommendations will be classified in this table according to their percentage of implementation and effectiveness.

Figure 1: Implementation of recommendations1

Proposed action	Implementation												Efficiency
	Month 1				Month 2				Month 3				
Lines of action	25%	50%	75%	100%	25%	50%	75%	100%	25%	50%	75%	100%	
													25%
													25%
													25%
													25%

In parallel, the second table will contain indicators that measure the effectiveness of the recommendations and their contributions to achieving the objectives set during the proposal of these actions.

Figure 2: Measurement indicators.2

Key results	Achievement of objectives			Objective
Key indicators				

As for the last table, it allows to identify the findings related to the effectiveness of the recommendations : based on this table, it can be deduced whether these recommendations will contribute to improving the accounting practices of the audited entity or, on the contrary, they prove to be useless and without added value.

Table 6: Findings of proposed actions5

Findings	Dedicated actions	Actors	Planning

Thus, the proposed dashboard in the context of this project proves to be very useful for both the audited entity, which will have all the necessary information regarding the effectiveness of the recommendations and their contribution to improving their internal control systems for better accounting efficiency, and for the auditor who will have the opportunity to evaluate the quality of their work to detect anomalies that require improvement and adjustment measures.

2-3-Complementary tool : the recommendation tracking sheet

I found it necessary to design this sheet as a complement to the previously proposed dashboard as it will facilitate the collection of information.

It is therefore an effective tool for permanent and immediate monitoring of the implementation of the actions recommended by the auditors.

The model I have chosen will only remain a fundamental basis, as it can be adjusted according to the needs of its user.

Indeed, this sheet contains all the information related to the title of the action and the references of the direct person responsible for its implementation. In addition, the table will allow to identify the gaps between what was planned in the auditors' report and what is actually achieved.

Furthermore, the particularity of this sheet lies in the provision of a specific framework to identify any obstacles that may hinder the implementation of the recommendations.

Implementation progress tracking sheet for recommendations

Tite of the action :

....
....

Action date

.........../.............../..........

Name of the responsable and hais/hier fonction :

....
....
....

Progress report on the action

Recommande action	Action implémente	Discrepancy	Observation

Possible challenges : The action has been slowed down or blocked

....
....
....
....
....
....
....
....

Specific observation

General conclusion :

The development of dashboards dedicated to the monitoring of recommendations constitutes a strategic innovation that goes beyond mere compliance with standards. These dashboards become essential management tools, allowing entities to fully benefit from the lessons learned from the audit to improve their governance and strengthen their performance. They provide a clear and concise view of the progress of corrective measures, enabling management to make informed and proactive decisions. Throughout the pages of this book, we have explored various aspects of the implementation and use of these dashboards. From advanced data analysis techniques to specifically tailored key performance indicators (KPIs), each component of the dashboard has been carefully designed to meet the needs of audit recommendation tracking. By focusing on clarity, simplicity, and relevance of the presented information, we have sought to create a dashboard model that is adaptable to various industries and company sizes.

The true advantage of these dashboards lies in their ability to transform audit recommendations into drivers of continuous improvement. By providing an overview of progress made and areas requiring special attention, these tools become catalysts for positive change. Managers can quickly identify trends, optimization opportunities, and areas where adjustments are needed, ensuring maximum utilization of resources.

One of the major contributions of this book also lies in the proposal of various techniques for tracking. Whether through report automation, data visualization, or integration of KPIs into daily management, each technique is part of a pragmatic approach aimed at simplifying tracking while maximizing its impact.

The importance of collaboration between internal teams and the external audit firm has also been emphasized. Audit recommendations should not be seen as a mere administrative formality, but as an opportunity to strengthen collaboration and mutual understanding. The joint development of tracking dashboards creates synergy that promotes alignment of objectives and consistency in the implementation of recommendations.

By adopting a value-added approach, organizations can transform the management of audit recommendations into a true strategic lever. Dashboards then become steering instruments offering a 360-degree view of performance, going beyond mere compliance to embrace a culture of accountability, transparency, and continuous improvement.

The relevance of the work lies in its ability to guide practitioners, leaders, and auditors in the concrete implementation of these dashboards. By providing concrete examples, adaptable models, and practical advice, it aims to make this innovative approach accessible to a wide audience. It is a comprehensive resource, combining theory with practice, to support organizations in their pursuit of excellence in financial governance. In conclusion, the development of a dashboard dedicated to monitoring the recommendations of a financial and accounting audit mission represents much more than a simple compliance step. It is a catalyst for organizational change, a gateway to continuous improvement, and a powerful tool for strengthening the trust of stakeholders. This work aspires to be a comprehensive guide for those seeking to embrace this innovative approach, offering a clear vision, practical advice, and tailored resources to make every audit mission an opportunity for positive transformation.

Appendix

Appendix 1: (Opinion Report)

OPINION REPORT ON FINANCIAL STATEMENTS PREPARED ACCORDING TO THE GENERAL CODE OF ACCOUNTING STANDARDS

Financial and accounting audit of company/establishment X
For the period from 01-01-2022 to 31-12-2022

Final Version

To Mr. Director,

To the Members of the Board of Directors of the company...

AUDIT OF FINANCIAL STATEMENTS

Qualified Opinion

In accordance with the mission entrusted to us by Contract No. 01/2022, we have conducted an audit of the attached financial statements of the company............, which include the balance sheet as of December 31, 2022, the income statement, the statement of retained earnings, the statement of cash flows for the year ended on that date, as well as the supplementary information statement (SIS). These financial statements show an amount of equity and similar items of .... MAD, including a net loss of .... MAD.

Subject to the impact of the situation described in the "Basis for Qualified Opinion" section of our report, we certify that the financial statements mentioned in the first paragraph above are regular and sincere and give, in all material respects, a true and fair view of the results of the operations of the past year as well as the financial position and assets of the Company as of December 31, 2022, in accordance with the applicable accounting framework in Morocco.

Basis for Qualified Opinion

The Company......... does not transfer the amount of the investment grant to operating income, for the portion that financed operations. In the absence of monitoring this transfer, we were unable to quantify the impact on the result of the year.

We have conducted our audit in accordance with the Standards of the Profession in Morocco. The responsibilities that are incumbent upon us under these standards are more fully described in the "Auditor's Responsibilities Regarding the Audit of Financial Statements" section of this report. We are independent of the company......... in accordance with the ethical rules applicable to the audit of financial statements in

Morocco, and we have fulfilled our other ethical responsibilities in accordance with these rules. We believe that the evidence we have obtained is sufficient and appropriate to support our qualified opinion.

Observations

We draw attention to the following facts:

1.
2.
3...

Our opinion is not modified with respect to these matters.

Responsibilities of management and governance officials regarding the financial statements.

The management is responsible for the preparation and faithful presentation of the financial statements, in accordance with the applicable accounting framework in Morocco, as well as for the internal control that it considers necessary to enable the preparation of financial statements free from material misstatement, whether due to fraud or error. In preparing the financial statements, it is the responsibility of management to assess the company's ability to continue as a going concern, to disclose, when applicable, matters related to the company's ability to continue as a going concern, and to apply the going concern accounting principle, unless management intends to liquidate the Agency or cease its operations or if no other realistic alternative is available. It is the responsibility of governance officials to oversee the company's financial reporting process.

Auditor's Responsibilities Regarding the Audit of the Financial Statements

Our objectives are to obtain reasonable assurance that the financial statements as a whole are free from material misstatement, whether due to fraud or error, and to issue an auditor's report containing our opinion. Reasonable assurance is a high level of assurance, but it does not guarantee that an audit conducted in accordance with the standards of the profession in Morocco will always detect any material misstatement that may exist. Misstatements may result from fraud or error and are considered material when it is reasonable to expect that they could influence the economic decisions that users of the financial statements make based on those statements. In the course of an audit conducted in accordance with the standards of the profession in Morocco, we exercise our professional judgment and maintain a critical mindset throughout the audit. In addition:

- We identify and assess the risks of material misstatement in the financial statements, whether due to fraud or error, design and implement audit procedures in response to those risks, and gather sufficient and appropriate audit evidence to support our opinion. The risk of not detecting a material misstatement resulting from fraud is higher than that of a material misstatement resulting from error, as fraud may involve collusion, forgery, intentional omissions, false representations, or circumvention of internal control;
- We obtain an understanding of the relevant internal control elements for the audit in order to design appropriate audit procedures in the circumstances, not for the purpose of expressing an opinion on the effectiveness of the company's internal control.
- ;
- We assess the appropriateness of the accounting methods selected and the reasonableness of the accounting estimates made by management, as well as the related disclosures provided by management;
- We draw a conclusion on the appropriateness of management's use of the going concern accounting principle and, based on the audit evidence obtained, on the existence or non-existence of a significant uncertainty related to events or conditions that may cast significant doubt on the company's ability to continue as a going concern. If we conclude that there is a significant uncertainty, we are required to draw the attention of the readers of our report to the information provided in the

financial statements regarding this uncertainty or, if such information is inadequate, to issue a modified opinion. Our conclusions are based on the audit evidence obtained up to the date of our report. Future events or conditions may also lead the company to cease its operations ;
- We evaluate the overall presentation, structure, and content of the financial statements, including the information provided in the ETIC, and assess whether the financial statements represent the underlying transactions and events in a manner that provides a true and fair view.
- We communicate to governance officials the planned scope and timing of the audit work and our significant findings, including any significant deficiencies in internal control that we have identified during our audit.

The Independent Auditor
………………………..
Date: …………………….

Bibliography :

- Hazami-Ammar, S. (2018). La contribution de l'auditeur interne à l'entreprise risk management : résultats d'une étude exploratoire. Recherches en Sciences de Gestion, 127, 107-133. https://doi.org/10.3917/resg.127.0107
- Portal, M. (2011). Les déterminants de la qualité de l'audit, le cas de l'audit des comptes publics. Comptabilité Contrôle Audit, 17, 37-65. https://doi.org/10.3917/cca.171.0037
- Lherm, F. (2013). Entre efficacité et légitimité : l'audit « scienctifié » et la dimension du croire dans le système financier. Nouvelle revue de psychosociologie, 16, 139-153. https://doi.org/10.3917/nrp.016.0139
- Savignat, P. (2014). Indicateurs, tableaux de bord, et mesure: Comment s'y retrouver ?. Dans : Jean-Yves Guéguen éd., L'année de l'action sociale 2015 : Objectif autonomie (pp. 217-230). Paris: Dunod. https://doi.org/10.3917/dunod.guegu.2014.02.0217
- DeAngelo, L. E. (1981). Auditor size and audit quality. Journal of Accounting and Economics, 3, 183-199. http://dx.doi.org/10.1016/0165-4101(81)90002-1.
- Chemingui, M., & Pigé, B. (2004). La qualité de l'audit : analyse critique et proposition d'une approche d'évaluation axée sur la nature des travaux d'audit réalisés. Post-Print halshs -00593012, HAL.
- Descheemaeker, P. (2003). "Nouvelle régulation internationale des sociétés cotées : les principales dispositions du Sarbanes-Oxley Act of 2002." Bulletin Joly Sociétés, janvier, 5-11.
- Hughes, M. (2003). "Some devil in the detail : Businesses could be underestimating their responsibilities on the need for internal controls under the Sarbanes-Oxley Act." Financial Times, 27 février, 2.
- Martin, D., & Robinson, G. (2002). "CEO and CFO certifications and new filing deadlines for annual and quarterly reports." Covington & Burling – Securities Practice Group.

- Cappelletti, L. (2000). Added value to the audited company provided by activity-based auditing process. Communication présentée au congrès de l'EAA (European Accounting Association).
- Bouquin, H., & Becour, J. C. (2008). Audit opérationnel: Entrepreneuriat, gouvernance et performance. Éditions Economica.
- Bernard, F., Gayraud, R., Rousseau, L. (2010). Contrôle interne, lutter contre la fraude : concepts, aspects règlementaires, gestion des risques, guide d'audit de la fraude, mise en place d'un dispositif de contrôle interne permanent, référentiels questionnaire, bonne pratiques… Paris: 3 Emme Edition Maxima.
- Agède, P. (1994). Habiller ses comptes. L'Entreprise, 106, 82-85.
- Adams, P., Cutler, S., McCuaig, B., Rai, S., Roth, J. (2012). Sawyer's Guide for Internal Auditors, Volume 3: Governance, Risk Management, and Compliance Essentials. IIARF.
- Barlas, S. (2003). Companies not excited about prospective internal controls report. Strategic Finance, 84(8), 23-24.
- Blanchet, A., Gotman, A. (2006). L'enquête et ses méthodes : L'entretien. Armand Colin.
- Bonner, S.E. and B.L. Lewis (1990). Determinants of Auditor Expertise. Journal of Accounting Research 28 (Supplement) : 1-28.
- Flint, D. (1988). The Philosophy and Principles of Auditing, Macmillan.
- Fortin, J. and L. Martel (1997). Enjeux éthiques de la réalité environnementale dans un contexte d'audit financier : une étude empirique. Comptabilité Contrôle Audit 2 (3) : 59-75.
- Thiery-Dubuisson, S. (2009). IV. Le contrôle des comptes : l'audit « final ». Dans : Stéphanie Thiery-Dubuisson éd., L'audit (pp. 71-92). Paris: La Découverte.

I want morebooks!

Buy your books fast and straightforward online - at one of world's fastest growing online book stores! Environmentally sound due to Print-on-Demand technologies.

Buy your books online at
www.morebooks.shop

Kaufen Sie Ihre Bücher schnell und unkompliziert online – auf einer der am schnellsten wachsenden Buchhandelsplattformen weltweit! Dank Print-On-Demand umwelt- und ressourcenschonend produziert.

Bücher schneller online kaufen
www.morebooks.shop

info@omniscriptum.com
www.omniscriptum.com

Milton Keynes UK
Ingram Content Group UK Ltd.
UKHW010037160624
444246UK00001B/40